Provinces and Territories of Canada

QUEBEC

— *"Je me souviens"* —

Published by Weigl Educational Publishers Limited
6325 10 Street SE
Calgary, Alberta
T2H 2Z9

www.weigl.com

Library and Archives Canada Cataloguing in Publication data available upon request.
Fax 403-233-7769 for the attention of the Publishing Records department.

ISBN 978-1-55388-976-2 (hard cover)
ISBN 978-1-55388-989-2 (soft cover)

Printed in the United States of America
1 2 3 4 5 6 7 8 9 0 13 12 11 10 09

Editor: Heather C. Hudak
Design: Terry Paulhus

Every reasonable effort has been made to trace ownership and to obtain permission to reprint copyright material. The publishers would be pleased
have any errors or omissions brought to their attention so that they may be corrected in subsequent printings.

Weigl acknowledges Getty Images as one of its image suppliers for this title.
Nasa: page 19 bottom; National Archives of Canada: page 29, 30 bottom.

All of the Internet URLs given in the book were valid at the time of publication. However, due to the dynamic nature of the Internet, some addresse
may have changed, or sites may have ceased to exist since publication. While the author and publisher regret any inconvenience this may cause
readers, no responsibility for any such changes can be accepted by either the author or the publisher.

We gratefully acknowledge the financial support of the Government of Canada through the Book Publishing Industry Development Program (BPIDP
for our publishing activities.

Contents

Quebec

Quebec's varied landscape makes it one of the most beautiful provinces in Canada. The incredible land is home to an abundance of animal and plant life. The province boasts clear rivers and lakes, lush forests, and rugged cliffs. Quebec was once covered with glaciers. These rivers of ice crept along grinding rocks, carving out wide valleys, and transporting soil as they moved. As the glaciers melted, the valleys filled with water to form thousands of sparkling lakes. Quebec is by far Canada's largest province in area. It is even larger than many countries in the world—Germany, France, and Spain could all easily fit inside Quebec's borders. Quebec also has the second largest population in the country, after Ontario.

Quebec is nicknamed "La belle province." This means "beautiful province" in English. The province has a total land area of 1,540,680 square kilometres. This is larger than the United States' largest state, Alaska.

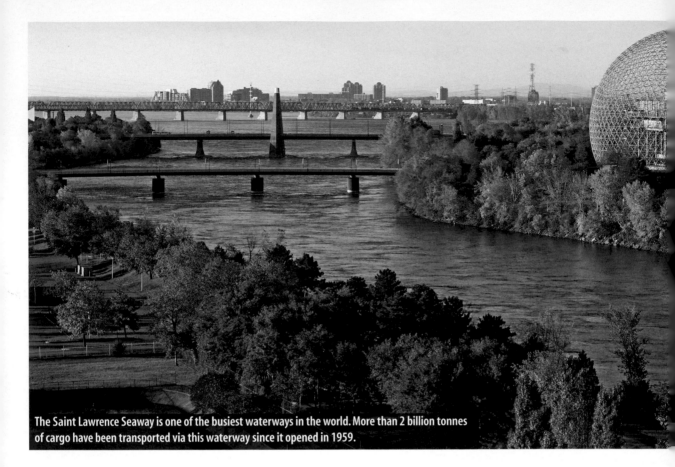

The Saint Lawrence Seaway is one of the busiest waterways in the world. More than 2 billion tonnes of cargo have been transported via this waterway since it opened in 1959.

Quebec is sandwiched between the Atlantic provinces and central Canada. Newfoundland and Labrador border Quebec to the east, and Ontario borders it to the west and south. New Brunswick also borders it to the south, as do the U.S. states of Maine, Vermont, New Hampshire, and New York. Water serves as the border for much of Quebec. Hudson Strait and Ungava Bay are to the north, while Hudson Bay and James Bay are to the west. The waves of the Gulf of Saint Lawrence crash against Quebec's southeastern shores.

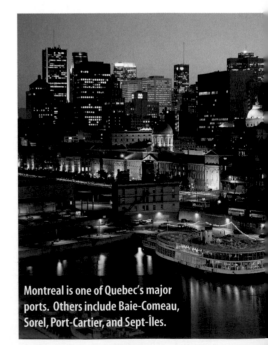

Montreal is one of Quebec's major ports. Others include Baie-Comeau, Sorel, Port-Cartier, and Sept-Îles.

Quebec's flag is the Fleurdelisé. It has a white cross on a blue background and a white fleur-de-lis flower in each corner.

The capital of Quebec is Quebec City. It is located at the mouth of the Saint Lawrence River.

Quebec's sparkling lakes and rivers provide excellent opportunities for outdoor recreation.

Most of Quebec's population speaks French, making it unique among the Canadian provinces. The French influence can be seen throughout the province. French-style homes line Quebec's streets, and schools preserve the ancestral language by teaching students in French. Street signs are usually in French as well as English. Quebeckers honour their French roots with festivals and celebrations throughout the year. They also work hard to preserve and celebrate their heritage.

GET THE FACTS

Quebec has about 28,000 kilometres of provincial roads and highways. About 70 percent of these are paved.

Many of the historic buildings in Quebec City reflect the classical architectural styles found in France.

Across the Ungava Bay and the Hudson Strait lies Nunavut, Canada's newest territory.

Quebec City is the only walled city in North America. It is also one of the few cities in the world that has been designated as a World Heritage Site.

The provincial motto is "Je me souviens." In English, this means "I remember."

Quebec received its name from the Algonquin. "Kebek" is an Algonquian word meaning "where the river narrows."

Quebec makes up more than 15 percent of Canada's total area.

LAND AND CLIMATE

The Montmorency Falls, near Quebec City, are 83 metres high. Roughly 35,000 litres of water flow over the falls every second. In the winter, the water freezes into a huge ice cone known as the "sugar loaf."

Quebec is made up of three land regions, including the Saint Lawrence Lowlands, the Appalachian Highlands, and the Canadian Shield. The Canadian Shield covers more than 90 percent of the province. It is characterized by many lakes and small hills, and neither people nor plants thrive in the harsh northern parts. Some of the rocks found in the shield are among the oldest in the world.

The Appalachian Highlands are to the south of the Saint Lawrence River. The highlands run from the Gaspé Peninsula south to Alabama in the United States. This region has many **plateaus** and valleys.

The Saint Lawrence Lowlands Region falls between the other two regions. It consists of Anticosti Island and the low-lying land of the Saint Lawrence River Valley. It is the heart of Quebec's successful farming industry.

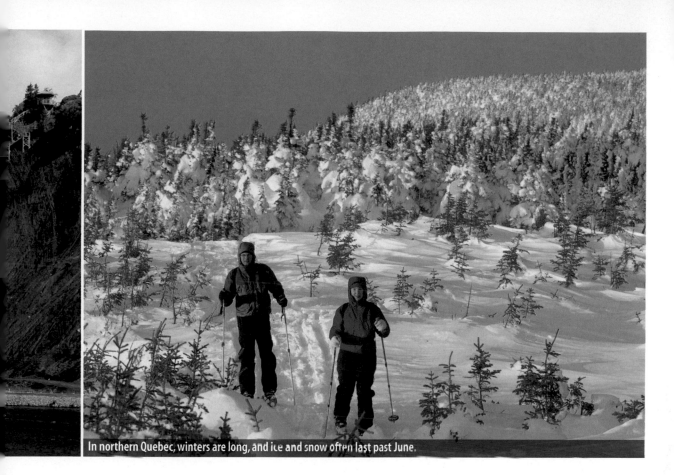
In northern Quebec, winters are long, and ice and snow often last past June.

Quebec's climate is greatly affected by wind. Winds from the North Pole sweep down across Quebec and over the most populated areas of the province. Heavy rain and snow falls where these cold winds meet the warmer air from the south. Unpredictable temperatures and long, cold winters are the result. Summers are often hot. Southern Quebec is humid, with about 1,000 millimetres of precipitation each year. Areas farther north experience colder and drier weather.

GET THE FACTS

The Canadian Shield is too cold for most crops. It is, however, rich in natural resources.

Îles de la Madeleine (Magdalen Islands), Anticosti Island, and Île d'Orléans are all part of Quebec.

The coldest temperature ever recorded in Quebec is −54° Celsius. The highest is 40° Celsius.

The Saint Lawrence Lowlands Region is the most fertile and most developed of Quebec's three land regions.

There are many lakes and rivers in the province. The most important waterway is the Saint Lawrence River. It is 3,700 kilometres long and flows into the Gulf of Saint Lawrence.

Quebec's highest point is Mont D'Iberville, at 1,652 metres.

NATURAL RESOURCES

Quebec makes more aluminum than any other province.

Quebec is rich in natural resources. It ranks third in Canada in non-fuel materials. Many resources and minerals are **refined** in Quebec, even if they were not mined there. Bauxite, which is a source of aluminum, is imported and refined. Zinc, iron ore, and copper are important natural resources mined and refined in the province. Iron ore is mined along the Quebec-Labrador border. These mines provide nearly half the country's supply of iron ore. There are also gold mines around Rouyn-Noranda and Val-d'Or.

 KEEP CONNECTED

Learn about aluminum and recycling at www.recycle. novelis.com/aluminumrecycling/Pages/Aluminum_ Recycling.aspx.

Quebec is the leading producer of maple syrup In the country. About 40 litres of tree sap is needed to make 1 litre of maple syrup.

Trees are another important natural resource in the province. Quebec has more forest than any other province in the country. Much of this land is owned by the provincial government. Some trees are used to make wood for construction, while others are used to produce maple syrup. Quebec's trees not only provide a boost to the economy, they also draw in tourists who want to enjoy the beauty of the province's forests.

GET E FACTS

The copper **smelter** in Rouyn–Noranda was built in 1922. It now employs over 800 people and processes over 300,000 tonnes of copper per year.

The area northwest of Montreal is rich in minerals such as magnesite, molybdenum, kaolin, graphite, and silica.

The Ungava Bay has become a leading nickel-copper-cobalt mining area.

Quebec is the world's leading producer of asbestos.

PLANTS AND ANIMALS

More than 25,000 different plant species can be found at Montreal's Botanical Gardens. These botanical gardens are the third largest in the world.

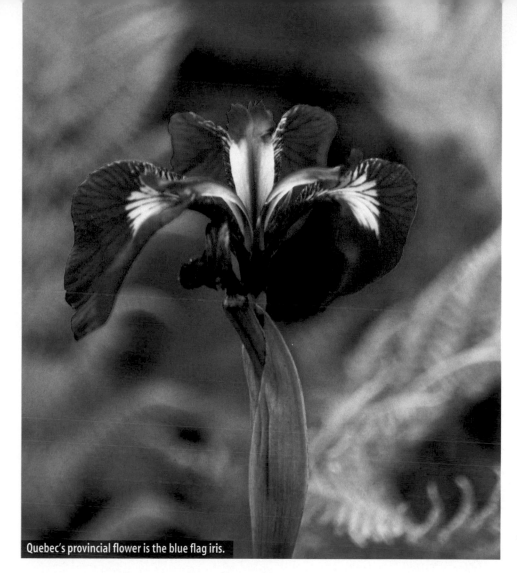
Quebec's provincial flower is the blue flag iris.

More than two-thirds of Quebec is covered with forests. Most of these are **boreal** forests with **coniferous** trees, such as balsam fir, black spruce, hemlock, and jack pine. Quebec's **temperate forests** lie south of the boreal forests. The **deciduous** trees in the temperate forests are mostly sugar maple, birch, elm, and oak. Parts of Quebec do not support much plant life at all. The extreme north is an area of **tundra**. This frozen land is home mainly to mosses, lichens, and low shrubs.

In the spring and summer, many of Quebec's forests are carpeted with wildflowers, including bellworts, bloodroots, dogtooth violets, trilliums, and spring beauties. Blue irises, goldenrods, and milkweed bloom throughout the province, while buttercups, daisies, prairie strawberries, and raspberries are found in Quebec's prairie lands.

Wolves are no longer found in southern Quebec. Coyotes have taken over the area, and the wolves have moved farther north.

From polar bears to beavers, Quebec is home to a wide variety of animal life. Large animals such as caribou, deer, black bears, and moose all live in Quebec's forests. Smaller animals in the province include skunks, raccoons, foxes, and squirrels.

A variety of birds are also found in Quebec. Some live in the province all year round. Snowy owls, chickadees, and sparrows are all permanent residents. The hermit thrush, ruffed grouse, Canada jay, and woodpecker are all found in Quebec's forests. Many other birds come to Quebec for the summer, then fly south for the winter.

The snowy owl has been Quebec's provincial bird since 1897.

There are about 500 beluga whales living near Quebec's shores.

Every year, thousands of caribou migrate between their summer feeding grounds and their winter forest homes.

The waters surrounding Quebec support a great deal of animal life. Whale-watchers keep their eyes on the Gulf of Saint Lawrence for signs of beluga and blue whales. Many different kinds of seals can also be spotted. The rivers and streams are full of fish, from northern pike and muskellunge to bass and trout. Atlantic salmon are abundant in the Saint Lawrence River's **tributaries**. Cod, mackerel, snow crab, shrimp, and lobster are all fished and harvested in the gulf.

Quebec's boreal forests cover a large portion of the Canadian Shield region.

More than 250 bird species can be seen at the Cap-Tourmente National Wildlife Area, east of Beaupré.

Quebeckers love to bird-watch. The province has more than 100 bird-watching clubs. Many people also have bird feeders at their homes, creating a successful birdseed industry.

More than 2,500 kinds of flowers grow in Quebec. This number is so high because of the vastly different habitats found in the province.

TOURISM

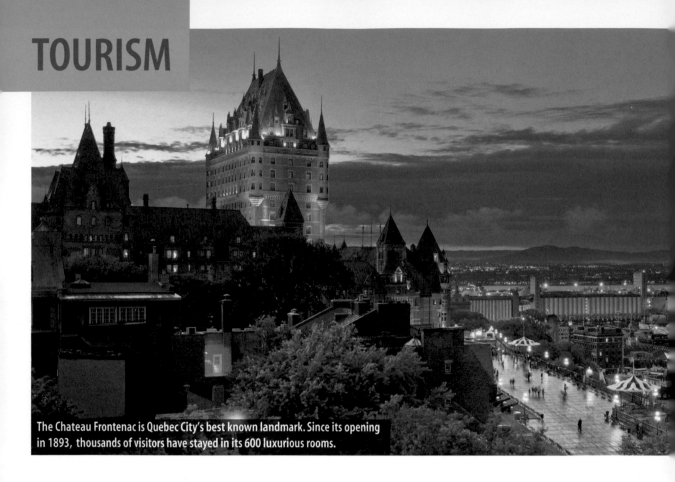

The Chateau Frontenac is Quebec City's best known landmark. Since its opening in 1893, thousands of visitors have stayed in its 600 luxurious rooms.

About 22 million tourists travel to Quebec each year to visit its historical landmarks and to experience its breathtaking scenery. Quebec City's cobblestone streets and old-French flair draw visitors from all over the world. Montreal also offers tourists historic attractions, as well as beautiful parks and unbeatable shopping. Many

The Canadian Museum of Civilization is located in Hull. This museum has more than 4 million artifacts relating to Canada's fascinating social history.

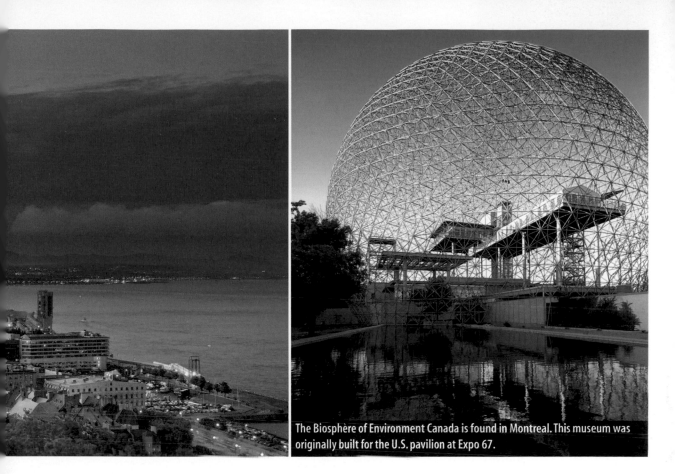

The Biosphère of Environment Canada is found in Montreal. This museum was originally built for the U.S. pavilion at Expo 67.

tourists visit the province to take advantage of the countless activities its lakes, rivers, and mountains have to offer.

History lovers have many attractions to choose from in Quebec. The Battle of Châteauguay National Historic Site holds re-enactments depicting the lives of the troops who fought during the War of 1812. Visitors to Fort Lennox National Historic Site, on Île-aux-Noix, can explore one of the largest forts in the country. The Citadel, in Quebec City, is also a popular attraction. It is the largest fort in North America still used as a military base. This star-shaped fortress was built in the late 1800s and has 25 buildings for tourists to see. It also has a museum that traces the province's long military history.

GET THE FACTS

The Battle of Châteauguay historic site commemorates the history of the only battle to take place in Quebec during the War of 1812.

Quebec has many fascinating museums. Among them are The Montreal Museum of Fine Arts, which holds collections of Canadian arts and paintings,

and the Musée national des beaux-arts du Québec, which exhibits Canadian art from as far back as the 1600s.

Saguenay River is used for hydroelectric power.

With all of the water around Quebec, it is no wonder that fishing is a major industry. There are about 40 fish-processing plants in Quebec. These plants provide fish lovers around the country with fresh, salted, smoked, and canned fish.

Water is also important to other Quebec industries. **Hydroelectric** power has become incredibly profitable in Quebec. This form of power supplies about 95 percent of the province's electricity. The enormous water reserves in the province make it relatively inexpensive for Quebec to generate hydroelectricity. Excess power is exported to the rest of Canada and to the United States. Quebec has become the leading producer of hydroelectricity in North America.

KEEP CONNECTED

More information about Quebec's fisheries can be found by visiting www.qc.dfo-mpo.gc.ca/index-eng.asp.

There are about 10,000 factories, mills, and refineries in Quebec.

The pulp and paper industry is important in Quebec. The province provides about one-third of all the pulp and paper produced in Canada.

Nearly half of Canada's aerospace industry is located in Quebec. It is the fifth-largest aerospace centre in the world. This industry produces airplanes, hydraulics, and **avionics**. Many of Quebec's successful aerospace companies are taking their expertise a step further in the satellite technology field.

GET THE FACTS

Most of Quebec's aerospace industries are based in Montreal.

Quebec is home to some of the largest hydroelectric power plants in the world.

Quebec's aerospace industry generates more than $8 billion for the province's economy and employs about 40,000 people.

Marc Garneau, from Quebec City, was the first Canadian astronaut to enter space. He flew on the space shuttle *Challenger* in 1984 and on *Endeavour* in 1996 and 2000.

GOODS AND SERVICES

There are about 40,000 farms in Quebec, mostly along the Saint Lawrence River.

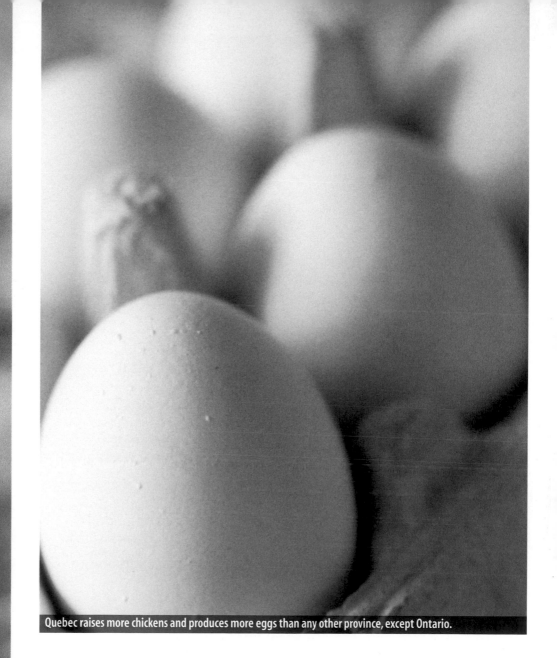

Quebec raises more chickens and produces more eggs than any other province, except Ontario.

Quebec produces many different agricultural products. Dairy products are among the most important—Quebec has the largest dairy industry in the country. Quebec dairy farmers produce delicious cheese, ice cream, milk, and butter. Most dairy cattle are raised in the Saint Lawrence Lowlands. This area has fertile soil that is ideal for grazing cattle and growing crops. Some farmers raise livestock. Pigs, beef cattle, sheep, and chickens are the most common livestock in Quebec. Other farmers grow crops, including corn, wheat, barley, oat, and soybean crops. Farmers also grow vegetables and fruits, such as potatoes, peas, lettuce, carrots, blueberries, and apples.

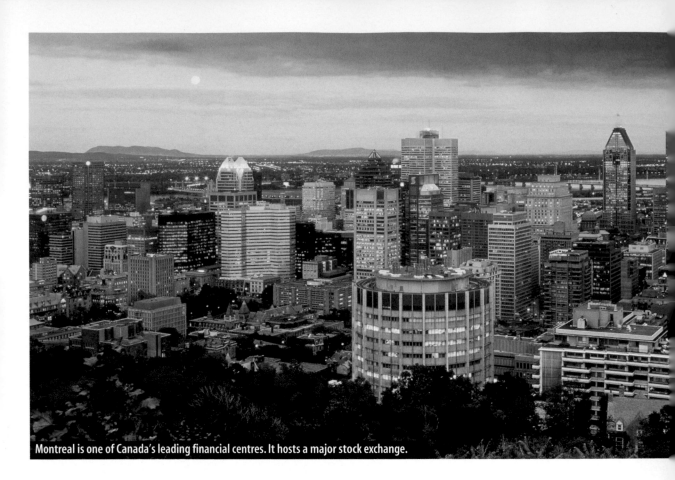
Montreal is one of Canada's leading financial centres. It hosts a major stock exchange.

Manufacturing employs about 19 percent of Quebec's workers. Most of the large factories can be found around Montreal. Food-processing plants throughout the province make pasta, butter, cheese, and soft drinks. Large bakeries and meat-packing plants are found in Montreal.

Chemicals are important manufactured products in Quebec. Industrial chemicals, toiletries, and **pharmaceuticals** are among the province's top chemical products. Quebec is a vital centre for pharmaceutical research and development in Canada. The province takes on about half of the country's production in this area. Many pharmaceutical jobs in research focus on **biotechnology**.

Information technology is a growing field in Quebec. Telecommunications equipment, electronics, and computer parts are produced in the province. More than 7,000 companies in this field operate in Quebec. This brings billions of dollars to the provincial economy and employs 100,000 Quebeckers.

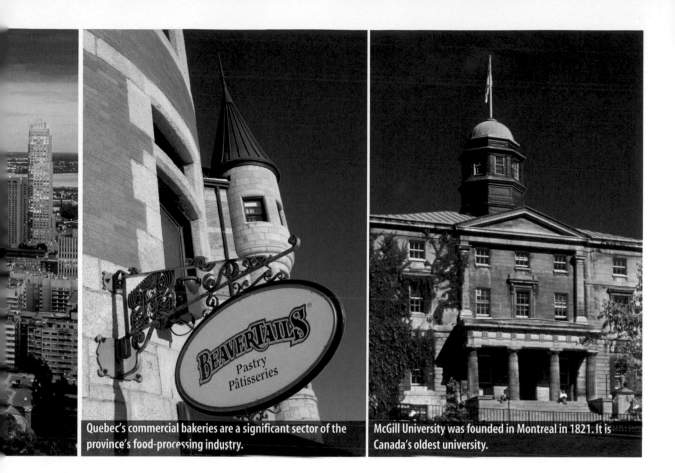

Quebec's commercial bakeries are a significant sector of the province's food-processing industry.

McGill University was founded in Montreal in 1821. It is Canada's oldest university.

The service industry is an important sector of Quebec's economy. Service employees do not create a product. Instead, they provide services for other people. These services include waiting on tables, taking reservations at a hotel, providing medical care, or selling goods at a store. Many people also work in the province's educational institutions, including its five largest universities—the University of Quebec, Laval University, the University of Montreal, McGill University, and Concordia University.

Students at the University of Montreal can take courses in a wide variety of subjects. The school has more than 250 undergraduate programs.

Many of the largest engineering research companies in the world are based in Montreal.

Canada's first radio broadcast was made in Montreal in 1919.

About 200 magazines and 250 newspapers are published in Quebec. Fourteen of these papers are published daily.

It is illegal for residents in Quebec to have personalized license plates.

About 85 percent of Quebec's international exports go to the United States.

FIRST NATIONS

The Iroquois is a confederacy of five groups. They are the Seneca, Oneida, Cayuga, Mohawk, and Onondaga.

Three main Aboriginal groups—the Algonquians, the Iroquoians, and the Inuit—lived in the Quebec area long before European explorers arrived. There were several groups in the Algonquian nation. Among them were the Algonquin, Attikamek, and Mi'kmaq. The Algonquin and Attikamek made their homes west of the Saint-Maurice River, while the Mi'kmaq lived on the Gaspé Peninsula. Many Aboriginal groups in Quebec hunted caribou and elk for food.

KEEP CONNECTED

Traditionally, the Iroquois lived in longhouses. To learn more about their ways of life, visit www.thecanadianencyclopedia.com. Type "Iroquois" into the search engine, and click on the first article.

Many early Inuit used dog power to get around. Dogsleds are still an important method of land transportation for Inuit today.

The Iroquoians lived mainly in the Saint Lawrence region. The good soil allowed them to farm. Crops supplied most of their food, making it easier for them to settle in one area. They built villages with permanent houses. Many of their longhouses were surrounded by **palisades** with fields of squash, corn, and beans growing outside them.

The Inuit lived in the north along Hudson Bay and the Ungava Peninsula. They relied on seals, whales, caribou, bears, fish, and birds for food, clothing, and shelter. Many Inuit preserve their culture and traditions by continuing their ancestors' methods of hunting and fishing.

GET THE FACTS

The Naskapi were hunters who lived in the east. The members of this group who lived farther south were called Montagnais, or mountaineers, by the French.

Iroquois women often planted, weeded, and harvested the fields. Men fished, hunted, and traded goods with other groups.

EXPLORERS

Iroquois from the Quebec region acted as interpreters and guides for Jacques Cartier as he explored the Saint Lawrence River.

E uropean explorers arrived in Quebec on their search for a water passage to Asia. In 1534, King Francis I sent explorer Jacques Cartier to claim the northern part of North America for France. He hoped this area would be rich in gold and other metals. Cartier explored Canada's coast and the river he called Saint Lawrence, but he did not find gold. He returned to the area in 1535 and travelled up the Saint Lawrence River to present-day Montreal Island. He then spent the winter in the village that later became Quebec City.

French fishermen fished along the coast and traded with the Aboriginal Peoples they met when they came ashore. The furs they took back to France increased the country's interest in Canada. In the 1580s, France started sending fur-trading expeditions to the Quebec region.

When Jacques Cartier reached Canada, he thought he had found gold and diamonds. However, when he brought his riches home to France, he was told his gold was worthless iron pyrite, or "fool's gold," and his diamonds were quartz.

In 1608, another French explorer arrived in Quebec. Samuel de Champlain built a trading post on the Saint Lawrence River. This area was called New France. Initially, few French people settled there. European companies were invited to become involved in the fur trade as long as they brought settlers.

Explorers traded guns, trinkets, kettles, and blankets with Aboriginal Peoples in exchange for furs.

Samuel de Champlain did not come to Canada alone. He brought Franciscan missionaries with him.

EARLY SETTLERS

Missionaries were some of the first people to arrive in New France.

Samuel de Champlain constructed this building in what is now Quebec City. The building housed a number of settlers and served as a storage facility for arms and provisions.

Settlement in New France came about slowly. In the 1620s, interest in fur trading was increasing. By 1628, a fur-trading company called the Company of New France planned to send about 400 settlers to the area. However, a war broke out between France and Britain, preventing many new settlers from moving to the region. Frequent battles for control of the North American colonies continued between France and Britain throughout the late 17th and 18th centuries.

Between 1635 and 1663, the population of Quebec's settlements began to grow. Schools and hospitals were built, and the colonies expanded. However, frequent attacks by the Iroquois had settlers in constant fear for their safety. Both the settlers and the fur-trading businesses were in danger. This prompted the French government to act. King Louis XIV began a new push to colonize the area. The king sent French troops to New France to defend against Iroquois attacks. In 1666, the troops invaded Iroquois settlements, burning crops and villages as they advanced. The Iroquois agreed to sign a peace treaty the next year.

On September 13, 1759, a monumental battle took place between the French and the British on the Plains of Abraham, outside Quebec City. After only 15 minutes, British General James Wolfe and his 8,500 troops defeated French General Louis-Joseph Montcalm and his 3,000 soldiers and 12,000 armed citizens. Both Wolfe and Montcalm were killed in the battle.

King Louis XIV then set up a French government in Quebec that was led by Jean Talon. Talon attracted thousands of immigrants to the area, and the population increased to 6,700 by 1672. Soon, farmers were harvesting enough food to feed their colony, with more for exporting or trading. Sawmills, tanneries, breweries, and a shipyard were built to take advantage of Quebec's natural resources. Despite this growth, settlers had many obstacles to overcome as they established their towns. Flooding, cold weather, crop failure, and supply ships intercepted by the British created many hardships. Hundreds of people were poor and hungry, and many had to work hard just to survive.

French settlers also had to survive the transfer of power from France to Britain. In 1760, after countless battles between the two nations, France was defeated.

Jean Talon was well respected among the province's early settlers, and New France flourished under his leadership.

New France had only 100 residents in 1627. Fewer than a dozen were women. By 1663, the population had increased to 2,500.

Under the 1763 Treaty of Utrecht, it surrendered almost all of its North American land to Britain. Many settlers resented British rule and were concerned that their French traditions would be threatened. Britain allowed them to have their own laws and their own systems of government in hopes that Quebec would be loyal. After many more wars and conflicts, Quebec's independence continued to develop.

By 1665, there were 1,300 French soldiers in New France.

In 1642, a group of missionaries established Montreal as a missionary settlement. While few settlers were eager to move to the settlement, it was an important fur-trading post.

The Company of New France had promised to establish a strong settler community in return for control of fur trading in the area. It did not live up to their end of the bargain. As a result, King Louis XIV dissolved the company.

Early settlers and Aboriginal Peoples had to fight against new diseases and illnesses in the 1750s. The hospitals were full with smallpox patients. Hundreds of people died from the disease.

POPULATION

The Gaspé Peninsula is the least populated region of Quebec.

More than 7.5 million people live in Quebec. The majority of the population lives in the southern part of the province. In fact, more than 80 percent of Quebec's population lives in an area that is 320 kilometres long and 97 kilometres wide, making it one of the highest concentrations of people in the country. Montreal and its surrounding areas are home to nearly half of the province's population. Quebec's other metropolitan areas include Chicoutimi-Jonquiere, Hull, Quebec City, and Trois-Rivieres.

There are more than 50,000 Aboriginal Peoples in Quebec.

About 88 percent of Quebeckers are Roman Catholics.

Most of the people in Quebec have French ancestry. French Canadians make up about 80 percent of the population. People of British descent make up about 10 percent of Quebec's population. The remaining 10 percent is made up of many Aboriginal Peoples, as well as other ethnic groups.

Montreal is by far Quebec's largest and busiest city. More than 3 million people live in the Montreal metropolitan area.

Montreal is the second largest French-speaking city in the world. The largest is Paris, France.

Until the 1940s, most of Quebec's population was rural. Now, only 20 percent of Quebeckers live in rural areas.

About 10,000 Inuit live in villages along the coasts of the Ungava Bay and Hudson Bay.

Since the end of World War II, about one million people from more than 80 countries have become Quebeckers.

POLITICS AND GOVERNMENT

Quebec's National Assembly has been meeting at Quebec City's Parliament Building for more than 100 years.

Quebec is governed by a 125-member National Assembly. The members are elected from wards throughout the province and serve five-year terms. The premier of Quebec is the head of the provincial government. The leader of the majority party is usually named premier. He or she has a council of ministers from the members of legislature. These ministers run about 20 departments of government.

Quebec has a different system of laws than the rest of Canada. It follows a system of civil law modelled after French civil code rather than English common law. In common law, cases are decided according to previous decisions. Quebec's judges decide according to rules of the civil code—they can disregard other decisions in similar cases.

Quebec has produced many important political figures throughout its history. In 1896, Sir Wilfred Laurier became the first French Canadian to serve as Canada's prime minister. He held the longest unbroken term as prime minister in Canadian history. Brian Mulroney was another Quebecker to serve as prime minister.

Louis St. Laurent's mother was English, and his father was French. This gave him a unique perspective on the country when he served as prime minister from 1948 until 1957.

"Trudeaumania" swept the country during Canada's 1968 election. Thousands of people attended Trudeau's rallies.

He won the biggest parliamentary victory ever, in the general election in 1984. Quebecker Jean Chrétien is from Shawinigan. He was the first French Canadian minister of finance in 1977, and became attorney general in 1980, and the opposition leader in 1990. Chrétien served as prime minister from 1993 to 2003.

Perhaps the most notable leader from Quebec was Pierre Trudeau. People adored this **charismatic** man. He was known for encouraging trade and for establishing constitutional independence from Great Britain in 1982. Trudeau retired in 1984. When he died in 2000, the country mourned the loss of a legend.

Canadian women could vote in federal elections by 1918, and most could vote in provincial matters by 1925. Thérèse Casgain successfully led Quebec women in demanding the right to vote in provincial elections in 1940.

Highly populated areas of Quebec are split into 95 regional municipalities. These are run by councils made up of elected mayors and alderpeople.

Quebec has 75 representatives in the Federal House of Commons and 24 members in the Senate.

Quebec was one of the four provinces that formed Canada on July 1, 1867.

CULTURAL GROUPS

Many Aboriginal groups make their homes in Quebec. Among the various groups are the Inuit, the Algonquian, and the Iroquoian. Many of these peoples live in one of more than 50 reservations throughout the province. They work to preserve and share their heritage and culture through traditional art, dancing, and ceremonies.

The largest cultural group in Quebec is the French. When the British controlled the colony's economy and government, Quebec's French people, called Québécois, maintained their own cultures and traditions. The community continues to preserve its culture. Some people in Quebec believe the province should be its own country. They want Quebec to separate from Canada because they feel their unique cultural heritage could be best preserved outside the country.

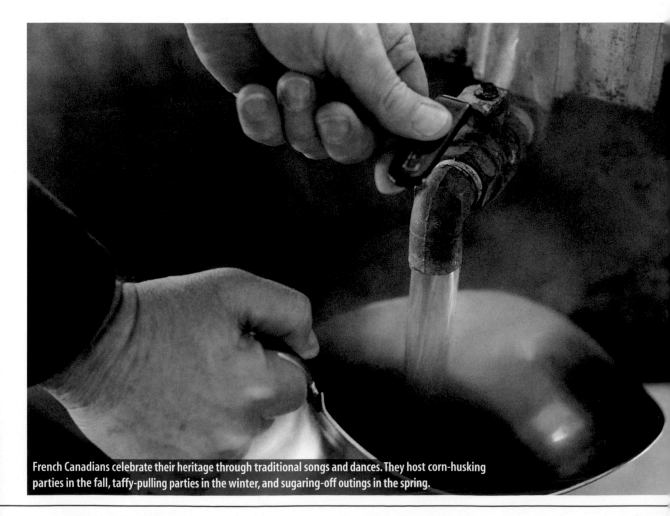

French Canadians celebrate their heritage through traditional songs and dances. They host corn-husking parties in the fall, taffy-pulling parties in the winter, and sugaring-off outings in the spring.

Since the early 1900s, many thousands of people have immigrated to Canada. People from Greece, Portugal, Germany, Hungary, and Armenia came to Quebec in search of a new life. Many immigrants from Asia and Latin America, as well as Caribbean countries including Haiti, also chose to live in Quebec. A large number of Italian and Jewish people have also made their homes in Quebec—mostly in Montreal. These ethnic communities have grown rapidly since the 1950s.

Many of Quebec's ethnic groups have created their own neighbourhoods. Often, the styles of their homes and gardens, and their shops and restaurants incorporate aspects of their homelands. Chinatown grew in Montreal after the railway was established in the 1860s. The construction of the railway employed many Chinese labourers. Today, Chinatown is a fascinating part of the city.

Montreal's Chinatown offers the tastes and sights of Chinese culture through its many stores and businesses.

European immigration brought people from England, Scotland, Ireland, and Italy to Quebec. American colonists who wanted their colonies to remain part of Britain also moved to the province to escape the American Revolution. They were called Loyalists.

GET THE FACTS

Many French Canadians are descendants of the original French settlers of the 1600s and 1700s.

There are more than 250,000 Italians living in Quebec. They are the province's second largest cultural group.

The Quebec City Summer Festival showcases African, French, and Quebec musicians.

Quebec's Jewish culture can be experienced at one of the many delicatessens, restaurants, or **synagogues** that are found in Montreal.

On June 24, French Quebeckers celebrate Saint-Jean Baptiste Day. This celebration honours Saint John the Baptist, the patron saint of French Canadians.

ARTS AND ENTERTAINMENT

Piano player Oscar Peterson won several Grammy Awards and became a jazz music legend. He started his career as a Montreal teenager and began recording his music at the age of 20.

Quebeckers like to entertain and be entertained. The province hosts nearly 300 festivals and carnivals every year. One of the most famous is the Winter Carnival in Quebec City. This annual event celebrates the season with the help of a snowman called Le Bonhomme Carnaval. For 17 days, Quebeckers enjoy parades, ice sculptures, and ice skating. To keep Montrealers laughing, the city hosts the largest comedy festival in the world. The Montreal Just for Laughs Festival features talented comedians from around the world and draws about 500,000 spectators to the city each year.

Quebec has produced many successful novelists. One of the province's best-known writers is Mordecai Richler. Much of his writing shows life as a Jewish Canadian in Montreal. His work for young readers, including his Jacob Two-Two books, have become must-read books for Canadian children from coast to coast.

All types of music can be heard throughout Quebec. The Quebec Symphony Orchestra has been entertaining listeners for nearly 100 years. Montreal's orchestra is known for its incredible recordings and highly

Playwright Michel Tremblay had a major impact on Quebec theatre in 1968. His characters talked in street French rather than formal French. His plays have been translated and performed all over the world.

Montrealer Leonard **Cohen** is a poet and novelist, but he is best known for his songs. In 1991, he was inducted into the Juno Awards Hall of Fame.

Céline Dion grew up in a large family. The youngest of 14 children, Céline began performing with her siblings at the early age of five.

The board game Trivial Pursuit was created by two friends in Montreal in 1980. The idea came to them in about 30 minutes, but they spent months researching the questions.

regarded conductors. For those who prefer popular music, Quebec is home to many talented pop stars. Corey Hart and Mitsou rose to fame in the 1980s. Kashtin was a duo consisting of Claude McKenzie and Florent Vallant. They were popular for their unique style of music.

One of Quebec's most celebrated singers is Céline Dion. She was one of the first singers to have incredible success in both English and French markets. This songstress from Charlemagne started singing professionally when she was a young girl. She has won several awards, including Felix, Juno, and Grammy Awards. Dion's beautiful voice was heard with her chart-topping song "My Heart Will Go On" in the blockbuster movie *Titanic*.

GET THE FACTS

Every August, the Montreal World Film Festival shows movies from dozens of countries.

Mordecai Richler is one of Canada's most respected authors. He has worked as a novelist, a journalist, and a screenwriter.

Les Grands Ballets Canadiens de Montréal is one of Quebec's major ballet companies. It is dedicated to performing ballets composed and choreographed by Canadians.

Anne Hébert was a Quebec poet and novelist who became famous for her novel *Kamouraska*. Her books were translated and enjoyed by English Canadians as well.

Some people enjoy sea kayaking near Perce Rock, Gaspé.

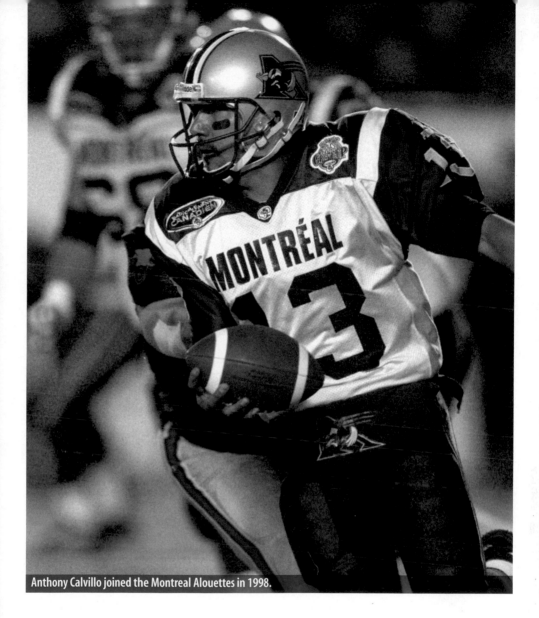

Anthony Calvillo joined the Montreal Alouettes in 1998.

Quebec's cold winters provide exciting sporting opportunities. Hockey, skating, snowshoeing, and skiing are all popular ways to spend a day. During the summer, residents can enjoy Quebec's beautiful scenery while swimming, bicycling, hiking, or canoeing. For those who would rather watch sports than participate, Quebec has thrilling action in the Canadian Football League and the National Hockey League.

Football fans in Quebec cheer for the Montreal Alouettes. The team disbanded in 1987 but made a return to the Canadian Football League in 1997. Alouettes fans look to talented footballers, including Anthony Calvillo, Randee Drew, and Damon Duval, to carry their team to the championships.

Today's Montreal Canadiens still bring fans out to cheer.

Perhaps the most popular professional sport in Quebec is hockey. The Montreal Canadiens have excited fans since 1909. The team boasts more championship wins than any other team in any sport in North America. Through the years, many Canadiens players have become heroes in Quebec.

Maurice Richard was a long-time fan favourite through the 1940s, 1950s, and 1960s. His explosive personality and his incredible slapshot earned him the nickname "The Rocket." He scored 544 goals in his career and was the first player to score 50 goals in one season. Jacques Plante was the team's goalie in the 1950s. In 1959, after being cut by a shot, he became the first goalie to insist on wearing a practice mask during games. This idea spread and led to present-day goalie masks.

Maurice Richard's incredible skill inspired the creation of a trophy given to the player with the most goals scored in a season. The trophy is named in his honour.

When she was 20 years old, goaltender Manon Rheaume made history. She became the first woman to play in an NHL hockey game. She appeared in an exhibition game with the Tampa Bay Lightning.

Jacques Villeneuve's father, Gilles, was known for his daring style of race car driving. He won the Grand Prix six times and died in 1982, when he collided with another car at the Belgian Grand Prix.

Sports fans who thrive on fast-paced action look to the racetrack. Quebec's Jacques Villeneuve is the province's best-known race car driver. He has won many races, including the Indianapolis 500. He also found success driving Formula One cars.

Gaetan Boucher won his first Canadian championship in speed skating when he was only 14 years old. He won three Olympic medals for Canada in 1984.

In 1995, the Quebec Nordiques hockey team was sold and became the Colorado Avalanche.

Lucile Wheeler was the first Canadian skier to win an Olympic medal. She took home a bronze medal in the downhill event in 1956. She was also the first North American to win a world championship, in both slalom and downhill, in 1958.

Hockey player Guy Lafleur led the Montreal Canadiens to five Stanley Cup victories and played from 1971 to 1991.

Myriam Bédard won two Olympic gold medals in the biathlon in 1994.

Hundreds of Quebec sporting groups organize activities in anything from **spelunking** to water-skiing to horseback riding.

GET THE FACTS

CANADA

Canada is a vast nation, and each province and territory has its own unique features. This map shows important information about each of Canada's 10 provinces and three territories, including when they joined Confederation, their size, population, and capital city. For more information about Canada, visit **http://canada.gc.ca**.

Alberta
Entered Confederation: 1905
Capital: Edmonton
Area: 661,848 sq km
Population: 3,632,483

British Columbia
Entered Confederation: 1871
Capital: Victoria
Area: 944,735 sq km
Population: 4,419,974

Manitoba
Entered Confederation: 1870
Capital: Winnipeg
Area: 647,797 sq km
Population: 1,213,815

New Brunswick
Entered Confederation: 1867
Capital: Fredericton
Area: 72,908 sq km
Population: 748,319

Newfoundland and Labrador
Entered Confederation: 1949
Capital: St. John's
Area: 405,212 sq km
Population: 508,990

SYMBOLS OF QUEBEC

FLAG   COAT OF ARMs   FLOWER
                                    Blue Flag Iris

Northwest Territories
Entered Confederation: 1870
Capital: Yellowknife
Area: 1,346,106 sq km
Population: 42,940

Nova Scotia
Entered Confederation: 1867
Capital: Halifax
Area: 55,284 sq km
Population: 939,531

Nunavut
Entered Confederation: 1999
Capital: Iqaluit
Area: 2,093,190 sq km
Population: 531,556

Ontario
Entered Confederation: 1867
Capital: Toronto
Area: 1,076,395 sq km
Population: 12,986,857

Prince Edward Island
Entered Confederation: 1873
Capital: Charlottetown
Area: 5,660 sq km
Population: 140,402

Quebec
Entered Confederation: 1867
Capital: Quebec City
Area: 1,542,056 sq km
Population: 7,782,561

Saskatchewan
Entered Confederation: 1905
Capital: Regina
Area: 651,036 sq km
Population: 1,023,810

Yukon
Entered Confederation: 1898
Capital: Whitehorse
Area: 482,443 sq km
Population: 33,442

BIRD
Snowy Owl

TREE
Yellow Birch

BRAIN TEASERS

Test your knowledge of Quebec by trying to answer these mind-boggling brain teasers!

1 True or False?

Quebec is the largest province in Canada.

2 Multiple Choice

Quebec is nicknamed "La belle province" which means what is English?
a) "province of bells"
b) "beautiful province"
c) "the best province"
D) "breathtaking province"

3 Multiple Choice

Which land region makes up 90 percent of Quebec's land?
a) Cordillera
b) Hudson Bay Lowlands
c) Canadian Shield
d) Interior Plains

4 Multiple Choice

Quebec has the largest _____ industry in the country.
a) dairy
b) cattle
c) rabbit
d) wheat

5 True or False?

Quebec is the leading producer of maple syrup in the country.

6 True or False?

Quebec is the world's leading producer of aluminum.

7 Multiple Choice

Which is one of the busiest ports in the world?
a) Shawinigan
b) Saint Lawrence Seaway
c) Hudson
d) Montreal

8 True or False?

Montreal is the second largest French-speaking city in the world.

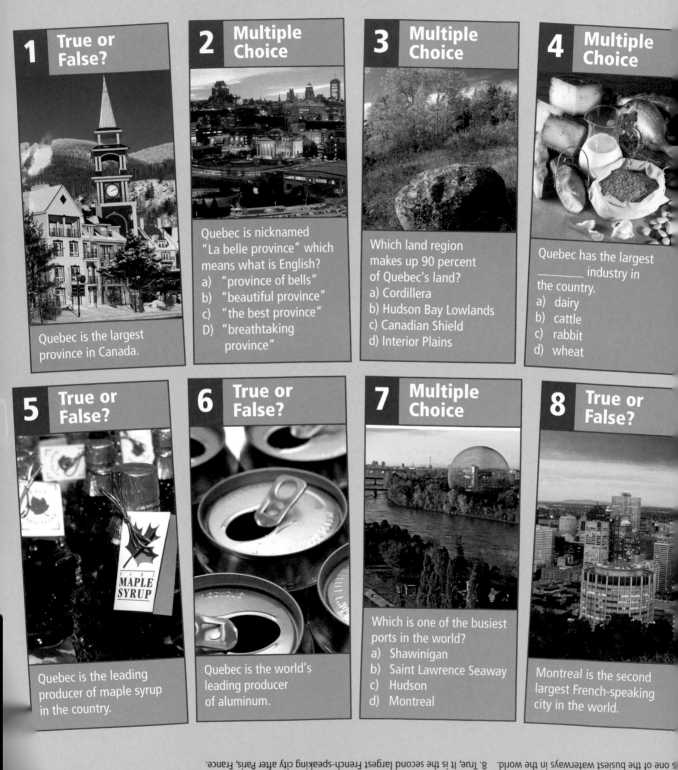

MORE INFORMATION

GLOSSARY

avionics: electronics used in aircraft and rockets

biotechnology: the use of biological processes for industrial purposes

boreal: large area in the northern hemisphere covered mainly in trees including pine, spruce, fir, birch, and poplar

charismatic: a person who charms and inspires great enthusiasm and devotion from others

coniferous: evergreen trees with needles and cones

deciduous: trees or shrubs that shed leaves every year

hydroelectric: energy produced by water power

palisades: fences made with pointed stakes

pharmaceuticals: medicines and prescription drugs

plateaus: level areas of land

refined: a substance that has had impurities or defects removed

smelters: places where ore is melted to obtain metals

spelunking: exploring caves

synagogues: buildings of public worship for those of Jewish faith

temperate forests: mixed and deciduous forests

tributaries: streams that flow into larger bodies of water

tundra: an arctic or subarctic plain with a permanently frozen subsoil

BOOKS

Craats, Rennay, *Canada's Land and People: Quebec*. Calgary: Weigl Educational Publishers Limited, 2008.

Craats, Rennay. *Canadian Sites and Symbols: Quebec*. Calgary: Weigl Educational Publishers Limited, 2004.

Foran, Jill. *Montreal: City of Culture*. From the Canadian Cities series. Calgary: Weigl Educational Publishers Limited, 2002.

Schwartzenberger, Tina. *Canadian Geographic Regions: The Canadian Shield*. Calgary: Weigl Educational Publishers Limited, 2006.

WEBSITES

Tourist Guide
www.quebecweb.com/introang.html

Montreal Canadiens
www.canadiens.com

Travel Quebec
www.bonjourquebec.com

Some websites stay current longer than others. To find information on Quebec, use your Internet search engine to look up such topics as "Montreal," "Quebec City," "Bonhomme," or any other topic you want to research.

INDEX